BEYOND BLACK AND WHITE

Elizabeth Rosalyn

BookLeaf
Publishing
India | USA | UK

Presentation by *BookLeaf Publishing*

Web: www.bookleafpub.com

E-mail: info@bookleafpub.com

ISBN: 9789358362077

First edition 2021

For those who want to make the world a more
compassionate and equal place to live in

1.

"Our conversations on issues of humanity and morality

Sway between black and white,

But it's the grey area

That begs the most urgency

For unpacking in our discussions.

Situations are more complicated than right or wrong.

We are more complex than good or bad.

Life is lived

In the light,

In the dark,

and in the in-between.

These conversations won't be easy,

But they need to be had

If we are to affect and achieve change.

With more listening and more understanding,

We can unlock the door to the grey room

And start to do better and be better."

2.

"One of the bravest things a person can do

Is to share art that comes from the heart,

And one of the best things a person can do to help someone

Is to help amplify the voices of others

So that they can express themselves and share their stories.

Through prose, poetry, and other forms of writing,

We begin to break down the barriers that block us

From fully understanding each other.

We begin to see how,

No matter how different our circumstances may be,

We are all alike in that

We experience ups and downs

Along the trials, tribulations, and emotional spectrum of our lives.

The more opportunities we have

To bridge the divide between people,

The better.

To be seen and to be heard

Is what every person deserves."

3.

"If you get knocked down

But refuse to stay down,

You can and you will

Rise Up

Stronger

and Higher

Than ever before."

4.

"Speak up.

Speak out.

Speak loudly.

Say your piece

To make your peace."

5.

"Look out for each other

Be aware of your impact

And strive for what benefits the world"

6.

"Be someone today

Who makes someone else

Look forward to tomorrow."

7.

"When you believe

No one is below you,

You will see

No one is above you."

8.

"To manage the varying states of mental chaos

We experience, day in and day out

In our everyday lives,

We need to be mindful of making

Our homes,

Our schools,

Our workplaces,

And other nests of gathering

Open,

Comfortable,

And safe spaces

For expressing the battles

We're waging in our minds.

Through conversation,

Through community,

We can ensure our time here

Is spent with care and compassion."

"I'm a believer in the notion of

Opening yourself up to

Random luck and accidental bumps

When you're out there living your life.

Embrace these regular injections

of unpredictable diversity.

Someday very soon,

You will meet new people

Who will teach you

Something new and profound,

Or maybe even change your life. "

10.

"Detours can lead you

To interesting places,

Interesting people, and

Interesting experiences.

Dare to venture off-road

A little more often."

11.

"A small comment can make

A big difference to someone.

Let's give each other

More compliments and sprinkle

A little more love and kindness

Into each other's lives. "

12.

"For those on the wrong side of human history, and yes, even those observing on the sidelines, right now, ask yourself:

How much more would we able to progress as a society if we dared to let go of our egos and our stubborn determination to win an argument, and instead, became interested in listening, really listening, to the thoughts and experiences of others without judgment?

What if we opened ourselves up to challenging our long-held and uncontested beliefs, and maybe even evolving our views? What if we saw this not as a sign of weakness, but as a sign of one's strength of character?

What if instead of fighting to always be right, we fought for the rights of others by calling out injustices and abuses of power in an effort to denormalize the behaviours and attitudes that threaten to set humanity backwards?

Especially for those who come from a place of privilege in society, listen, REALLY LISTEN, to those who come from different backgrounds, upbringings, cultures, and lived experiences as you. And use your position of privilege to fight for their right to have a voice and to be heard.

When lives are at stake, it's not the time for apathy. It's the time for action.

Evolution is the revolution."

13.

"Every time you thought

You couldn't go on

And move forward...

Remember,

You did."

14.

"In this wild world we've living in,

Where getting through one day

Can feel like an uphill battle,

Experiencing the giving and receiving

Of genuine gestures of gratitude

Can make a day when it feels like

Everything is breaking down.

When you know this,

A "thank you" and a smile

Become powerful means of lifting

Someone's entire perspective and direction."

15.

"What's inevitable is that

You will fail at being

Who you're supposed to be.

Instead,

Measure yourself by

How well you succeed

At being who you are."

16.

"Life is a constant journey

Of self-discovery.

You can never know exactly

Who you are,

Or who you will become.

But in your journey of evolution,

You become more comfortable in discomfort"

17.

"To be seen is

To be elevated,

Tofeel your spirits lifted,

And to be raise one's belief in their worth.

Be bold in giving

Love and kindness daily.

Don't underestimate

Your impact on people,

For you have unlimited potential

To uplift someone."

18.

""I believe in you"

Are the best words

You can give to someone,

And to yourself."

.

"How to be a better ally:

See colour.

Check your privilege.

CONFRONT IT.

Do the work.

Educate yourself.

LEARN.

Amplify the voices of BIPOCs.

Have uncomfortable conversations.

LISTEN.

Call out racist comments.

Challenge microaggressions.

PAY ATTENTION.

Speak up.

Stand up.

DO BETTER."

20.

"Before all else,

Give grace to yourself.

Because with deeper self awareness and acceptance

Comes a greater understanding

Of the people and the world around you.

To be of compassionate service to your purpose,

You need to surround yourself with love and kindness

In your inner world as well."

www.ingramcontent.com/pod-product-compliance
Lightning Source LLC
Chambersburg PA
CBHW071246140726
47996CB00007B/2772